Stopping for Breath

Also by Norita Dittberner-Jax

What They Always Were
The Watch
Longing for Home

Stopping for Breath

poems

Norita Dittberner-Jax

NODIN PRESS

Design: John Toren
Cover photo: Norita Dittberner-Jax
ISBN: 978-1-935666-70-7
Library of Congress Cataloging-in-Publication Data

Dittberner-Jax, Norita.
[Poems. Selections]
Stopping for breath / Norita Dittberner-Jax.
pages ; cm
ISBN 978-1-935666-70-7
I. Title.
PS3554.I8397A6 2014
811'.54--dc23
                            2014032110

Nodin Press
5114 Cedar Lake Road,
Minneapolis, MN 55416

For my people

the living and the dead

A deep breath,
the beating
of rain on the sill,
ground
under my feet,
eyes open.
I know the world,
cousin to water
to air temperate
against skin,
the steady
heat of low fires,
and always,
the earth.

CONTENTS

Stopping for Breath

SUPERIOR AT THE SHORELINE: FEBRUARY

Think of it as a kingdom of ice,
its vast depths, turbulence in check,
the beach you walked,
the red umbrella you planted
in the sand, lost.

But find a spot, dig your boots
into the snowpack. Bring the quiet
you kept while the baby
slept, that cathedral silence.
Watch the lake begin to breathe
at the seams, the slight rise and fall
of its breast, the deep push
against ice, the first crack.

It will be weeks before it gains
strength at the shoreline to blast
the rocks on which you stood as a girl,
stunned by its fierce rhythm,
in love with it, as young girls love
the galloping horse.

MEDITATION

How to manage
the hours, the hands
of the clock
that seem
to stick sometimes,
and lurch
ahead at others?
Without a compass,
she is hollow,
an empty
barn with the wind
tunneling though.
Toward evening,
an easing,
breath deepens,
waves of anxiety
melt away, as if
the trouble were in nature.
The sun slides
toward the horizon,
sending vibrations
through the sky,
casting shadow.
The trees,
her beloved trees,
ghostly at twilight,
keep their shadows close,
a comfort,
the reality of ghosts,
finally visible,
a brief appearance
of the truth
before night covers all.

CROSSING

On my lunch hour, I stepped off
the curb at the green light, thinking
of the evening to come with you.

A shaking came over me.
I felt my body changing
as if I might be a tree,

not Daphne fleeing Apollo.
This was a welcoming,
the hour of attachment,

life shooting through me
from root to crown,
a shimmering crossing with no

turning back.

FOSSIL

They found her
in the Ethiopian desert
once verdant with palm
and fig, she among the fossils
of shrew and bat,
rhino, giraffe.

Hippos trampled her bones;
millions of years later,
fragments surfaced,
which, when touched,
turned to biblical dust.

Under the microscope,
she emerges,
millimeter
by millimeter.

She is a shape I recognize—
smooth breasts, flaring
pelvis, thick pubic hair.

Gorilla, chimpanzee,
the whole order of monkeys,
fingering food, wiping
their faces, gestures
mirroring mine.

In the newspaper drawing,
she looks straight at me
as if to say, *here I am,*

one hand open
like an early photograph
of my mother.

Ungainly hands and feet,
no embarrassment
about their size.

I think of the life of women,
of my life, with all
its accoutrements.

Dust, all turned to dust,
the line of ancestors
at the root of the family tree.

I keep the drawing close.

I WRITE

for the woman who stares out the window at the oak tree
but does not see it so she sees it.

for the oak trees who go right on being shaggy and helpful
and no one thanks them.

for the man who asked me about my poems and I asked
him about his horses and the horses and the poems were
the same.

to keep alive the memory of my mother, father, brother,
sister. I write for the dead to go on living.

to keep myself alive; without it, I'm just grinding coffee,
shuffling papers, turning in sleep.

for the moments when I step into a pool of light
and know it.

ROAD TO THE SEA

Alone, today
I go to the sea where I lived
in an earlier life.

Descending through mountains
I stare at them the way villagers
stare at me: *Who are you?*
What form of life?

Mountain folded into mountain.
The driver weaves around
them, they make room, but only
a little.

Bulbous, ungreened.
I call them grandfather.
The sea, I call mother.

CROSSING THE EQUATOR

I woke up
and saw the Southern sky.
We were flying a plateau
of pure color,
a heavenly blue
that cut a swath of clarity
far above weather.
On the belly of blue,
the blue of whales
and morning glories,
hung the moon,
a sliver of pure light,
its position strange,
as if some gravitational
pull had tipped it to rights,
a cap of glorious light,
ends pointing perfectly
toward earth; stars gathered
around this moon
in configurations
new to me.
I awakened to light.

FAMILY ALBUM

1.
My sister loves the photograph
of the first five children of our family.

It is a beautiful portrait, the youngest standing
in his sailor suit on a pedestal.

She goes on so lovingly that I say, "It would have been nice
if there were a photograph of all of us."

I feel small saying this, but I want to stand up
for my brother and me. Even now with my hair

graying fast, I'm saying, "Push over! Make room!"
Five children in a row, a hiatus, then two more.

Mother was 46 and 48. A few snapshots. Dad driving
truck, all those mouths to feed.

2.
My mother told me,
"We hadn't had a baby
for awhile; you were
the most wanted baby."

Years later, when I told a counselor,
she said, "You believed her?"

3.
You can tell the sashes of her dress are torn
the way the waist hangs lose on her skinny frame.

There's a ribbon in her hair, tight curls from
the Toni permanent her mother gave her

at the kitchen table one Friday night
while her father watched the boxing matches

and the house rang with the clang of each round ending.
Otherwise that hair would be straight as a plumb line.

There's a big bandage on her left arm from some mishap,
but that smile, the light in her eyes, that girl is glad

to be alive and sitting on the piano bench with her little brother
in short pants, palms on his kneecaps, looking up, enchanted,

the older five behind them, but no one happier than these two,
who knew it could have been otherwise.

HERE

I can't speak for elsewhere
but here the sun rises and sets
and sometimes you can't see it.
Gravity pulls us toward earth
which spins so slowly, you can't
feel it. Sometimes it's cold,
sometimes, hot. It sounds simple,
but the effects are dramatic—
Trees stand like bleak sculptures
for months then suddenly break
out into leaves with tiny veins
you can feel with your fingertips.
Like the nerves in the body
that power your fingers and
everything else unless you have
a stroke, an explosion in the brain.
Then you can't feel the veins of
the leaves or even sorrow you felt
last week. I can't speak for elsewhere
but here, you get used to one thing,
then it's another, like day and night,
and you want someone to answer for it.

MOUNTAINS

When she described the mountains
it was a with a farm girl's wonder,
a trip out West to the Rockies,
a last fling before marriage.

She didn't know seven children
would follow, a life, hard-scrabble
and rich. When I see them, I'm breathless
as she must have been, the dizzying air
of the vertical, something like God.

She came to sit with the children
and afterwards, we talked in the kitchen,
the table between us, warming our hands
around cups of coffee.

SIGHTINGS

Rabbits on the boulevard
are a sign of God's presence.

Night terrors, the visitation
of God's angel, keeping you real.

The stubborn intractable presence
of the poor, God-with-us.

The first breath and the last,
God's portion.

Fra Angelico's "Annunciation,"
the God-particle in the artist.

God in the stance of the oak,
the surge of life upward.

In the child hiding from an embrace,
God's love coming forward.

In the multiplicity of bugs, insects, birds,
God with an appetite.

God in the softening of sorrow,
the throwing up of hands in defeat.

God in the pulse, heartbeat
of the universe.

God in the fragments.

after Anne Carson

EVENING

Sweetness of lilac in the empty schoolyard

First cut of grass, blades lifted
by a wind, soft as an arm
around my shoulder.

STATUE

In the Church of Saints Cosmos and Damien, there
is a statue, a group of four figures—a saint in the
background holding a sheaf of wheat, a team of oxen,
an angel behind the team holding the handle of the
plow. A tableaux, a scene, but what is the story? Who
has an angel do his work? What remarkable good has
this saint done that the angel has intervened? I try to
imagine that story, but my mind goes back to the oxen
who outweigh the others, although the man is well-
formed and the span of the angel's wings impressive.
Still nothing equals the structural beauty of the oxen,
heads tapering to nose and the scaffolding of shoulders
bearing the weight forward.

PHOTO

An old negative
never developed
until now: my parents,
ready to walk me
down the aisle
our arms linked.

A poor picture
of my mother,
a good-looking woman,
but here, tired.
My father, handsome,
vibrant as I am.

I cut my mother
out of the photo.
I am pretending
my father and I
were pals. Picture me
with my mother
in a hundred ways,
dancing her around
the kitchen, she,
in her apron. Later on,
in the wheelchair.

There is no photo
of father and daughter
like this, so I made one,
and here we are,
both of us dressed to the nines
a white blaze of orchids
between us.

RAIN

Sheets of rain, soak of April,
heavy-falling-down water
running like thieves through the street.

I was born in this month.
When my mother brought me home,
the soles of the children's shoes

were eaten away by the downpour.
Cardboard soles, the rationing
of leather during the war.

Later, my dad took me to Schloff's
for sturdy brown oxfords which would not
disintegrate under any conditions.

Today I smelled the rain-on-dirt smell
fat drops hitting hard scrabble, rain soaking
thick thumb weeds in empty corner lots.

MY DAD COMES BACK ON GRAND AVENUE

He bought big for the family, crates full
of peaches from the wholesaler,
meat from the butcher in blood-stained apron.

I followed him up the steps,
watched him bargain, the good-natured
barbs, a way to be with him.

He relished the give and take of it,
the basic transaction of commerce,
I have what you need.

About my street, he'd think, what a waste,
pots of flowers at the door of the boutique,
and who needs an olive oil shop?

He's come back in the easiest
way I knew him, making small deals,
at ease in the world.

What he had to teach me took hold
though I wanted more.

I walk the street, cheerful and suspicious
as he was, wondering what nefarious
deed shut down the restaurant,

leaving the tables set,
napkins fanned like swans
swimming a white sea.

In Memoriam

for Jim White

You died sometime Sunday night
before my letter arrived. It came back marked,
"Return to Sender. Deceased."

My time was Tuesday at 4:00, $15 in cash
to sit at your kitchen table
sipping sassafras tea while you read my poems,
one you marked, *lofty.*

"Write about Frogtown," you told me,
"write about coal yards and railroad tracks,
laundry flapping the clothesline."

What a dowsing that was, a strike deep
into the ground where real poems lived.
Feverish, I wrote you a letter so we could begin.

You were buried like a nobleman.
We sang you out with stout
Episcopalian hymns in the cathedral
and a feast of funeral food
for a lover of sweets.

The great wheel moved forward,
implacable beast,
dumb to your gifts.

Jazz Trumpeter

"You are not who this country says you are."
— Hannabal Lakumbe

His voice is soft
and he stops often.
The young black men
around the table,
fidget with their braids,
sprawl.

Doing the right thing
he says, is harder
than a hundred Chinese push-ups.
A pause for push-ups.
The boys take turns
making the triangle
with their hands on the floor,
getting their chins down
into that triangle.

He wears them down
with his voice,
his silence. He waits
for them to find their way
and they do: one
tells of the grandmother
related to Ida B. Wells,
another to Leadbelly.
None of these boys
is nothing.

On their faces,
a sense of calm
as if some confusion
has been ordered,
hands quiet in their laps.

He takes up the trumpet,
the slow wail,
shows them what to do
with sorrow.

HOLDING THE MOMENT

Between two lions,
yesterday and tomorrow,
how narrow, today.

CITY TREES, COFFEE SHOP, SPRING

Some days trees are all I see.
Today they're getting fringed in leaves
at the crown. Underneath
there's a huge ball of root that nobody sees
except my son as a five-year old
who drew one exactly as a botanist might,
side view, x-ray vision.

Nobody talks about trees over cappuccino.
Outside the coffee shop, friends
laugh about Friday night's game.
A jogger passes me; a car horn shrieks.

Let this Saturday be perfect.
Let nothing terrible happen.
No stray bullets or pedestrian deaths.
Let traffic roll safety toward the freeway.
Let the trees survive, let them be
counted, cared for, oldest residents of the city.

TRAVELING OUT:
A MIDWESTERNER'S LOVE OF WATER

> *"I gave my imagination to water,*
> *the green, clear water."*
> – Gaston Bachelard

Flying over the Atlantic Ocean, a whole mountain range
underneath; how many miles to the foot of the mountain?

Amazon River, the flowing together of the River Negro
and the River Solimoes, dolphins leaping at the point of
confluence.

Black Sea, choppy waters, the boat we rode with
Istanbulis pointing to mosques on shore
like fabulous baubles.

Canals circling the city of Amsterdam, boats and bikes
parked at the dock of each house.

Columbia River, deep gash in the earth; Chippewa
River and Chester Creek, minor bodies of water where
daughters blossomed.

Como Lake, the concordance of duck and geese, first
visit at ten days old, last, just yesterday.

Dead Sea, the day we lost each other. Feeling stupid
floating in the water, the itch of salt. From the bus
window, Bedouins riding camels over sand dunes.

The great biblical rivers of Mesopotamia, Euphrates and Tigris, the land between, source of the garden. Always in my mind. How many times did we see fire exploding the banks of Eden?

Galway Bay, source of song and story, why the Irish long for home.

Ganges, sacred river of India, not seen, but revered of souls. In the same alphabet as Gull Lake, all of us happy on its shore.

Hudson River and East River, how their long arms embrace Manhattan.

Itasca, origin of the Mississippi, a seed, an idea that grew to run straight down the middle of the country.

Saint Lawrence River at its most beautiful in Quebec, the Plains of Abraham, artery to the heart of North America.

Mekong River of lives lost and found, the Hmong, their very bodies the boats families rode to safety.

The Moldau in Eastern Europe, old river of wedding cake Prague.

Mediterranean Sea known to me only from Odysseus until I rode its waves in Barcelona.

Mississippi River, my river, where God got the idea for river, and little McCarrons, lake of terrible sunburn, little blond girl in the lake all day.

Nile River, not seen, but how I envied you, husband, riding it, you and Cleopatra.

The Potomac and the Pacific, the seat of power and the power.

Q, also U, also Z. An absence. Will I see them?

Red River of the North, river of historic floods and fertile farmland, flat, black gold.

Lake Superior, dark and wild, endless pleasure for the eye, home of beloved grandsons.

The Seine, river of Paris, imperial white bridges, how brilliant the blue nights.

The noble rivers of T: the Thames, a dream, flowing past the Houses of Parliament, but higher up, Virginia Woolf's back yard, where she weighted herself down with stones.

The Tiber of Rome, guarded by gods and Renaissance angels, pigeons perched on their wings.

Tagus, tidal river of Portugal, the launching of ships to the new world at high tide.

The Volga of Russia, Moscow, river of tsars and communists, of Stalin and Putin, river of revolutionaries and bureaucrats.

Wisconsin River, meandering river of canoes and fishing, of willows bending over its waters, my husband's river.

The Yangtze, great river of China, not seen except in *The Story About Ping*, "A beautiful young duck lived with his mother and his father and two sisters and three brothers and eleven aunts and seven uncles and forty-two cousins in a boat with two wise eyes on the Yangtze river."

Bodies of water rock me to sleep.

after Robert Pinsky

THE BLESSING OF THE TUNA FLEET AT GROIX

Signac painted the fishing boats straight on,
Five of them and a little skiff,
prows forward, masts splicing the air,
flags flying in the breeze of a most
temperate day, clouds, but no rain, the rippling
Atlantic waters contained in the bay.

The people, sticks of black behind the boats,
barely visible, but I bet the whole town
turned out for the send-off, at least one child
fished out, gasping, and the priest, rushing
the planks, wings of his stole flapping
behind him, ready to fling holy water aloft.

But the blessing belongs to the artist
who must have sketched the scene from his own boat
further out, the one he sailed from Mediterranean
port to port, all the way to Istanbul.
He painted a thousand dabs of color
he knew the eye would transform into fish for the catch.

MORNING

The smell of earth, of moisture and dirt after rain,
sparrows in the oak, the acorns which drop
like hailstones on the roof.

In the garden, prodigious weeds and a foxglove bending
under the weight of its bells. The alley cat still
homeless.

In the schoolyard across the street, workers seed
new grass for the recess to come.
The east side of everything illuminated.

THE ONLY THING THAT HAPPENED IN 4TH GRADE

Afterward, I never wanted to be fat again.
Frank and I had to wash the blackboard
before the bell rang at St. Vincent's.

We stood with our backs to the others
at the board, erasing the chalk dust,
then dipping our sponges in the bucket

of water, *working off the weight*, she said.
We tried not to leave stripes, to leave
no trace of the day's lessons.

It was private, eyes only, Frank and me,
and the others watching. Do they remember?
Does Frank? Even writing this,

I see the lie in the plural—*Frank and me,
we, us*. In the cloakroom of shame,
there is always only one small child.

Waiting for the Year to End

Time was a stuck clock striking the same hour
over and over. I was the minute hand wanting to move.

Simon and Garfunkel sang the bridge song while I
nursed the baby, nipples cracking.

Bombs exploded and the roll call of the dead smelled
like ash on the living room floor.

This was before Nixon waved from the helicopter
on the way to San Clemente.

I was a good Catholic girl trying to do the right thing
in the wrong year. My mother stroked out that autumn.

The doctor shrugged his shoulders. He was the boatman
rowing under the bridge of trouble.

When the soldiers invaded Cambodia, we marched down
Summit Avenue with the draft resisters.

"Hell, no, we won't go!" The flag hung on the hour hand of
the clock. I caught the baby before she climbed the fence.

On Christmas Eve, we took the children to a peace
vigil they do not remember.

Death strolled among us, staring out of his black-
hooded skull. We were used to him by then.

SOLDIERS' FIELD

"We Have Died. Remember Us."
– Archibald MacLeish

Before my brother was buried here,
I drove past the cemetery,
hill after hill of identical gravestones,
like the stars on the flag.
Now I enter the grounds and find
his name carved on white stone.

I was ten when he went into the navy,
a sailor in dress whites, cap angled
on his head. He brought our mother
Japanese china that dressed up
the dining room table ever after.

Since his death, I've been collecting
photos, pouring over Veteran's Day
snapshots of soldiers lined up
like seniors in a year book:

A sailor from World War II,
face blurred, as if moving through fog,
eyes pierced with dread.
A good-looking soldier from World War I
pencil mustache, perfectly groomed.
A Civil War photo of George Custer
lounging in the grass outside his tent,
petting a dog.

I collect facts too. During the Civil War,
the stonecutters couldn't keep up
with the loss of lives. Now machines
do the work, cutting letters precisely
into white marble. We do these things
fast now. It's an industry.

My brother's stone was ready in three weeks.
He served in the Korean Conflict.
It's hard to keep the wars straight
if you use the same word. He rests
with thousands of others in a soldiers' field
near the airport where planes taking off
rock the ground they're buried in.

SISTER

1.
Inside the door of the hospital
dozens of wheelchairs
abandoned like bumper cars
at the fair.

Everyone I see is brown-skinned:
the clerk at the desk who waves me on—-
the cleaners moving silently,
their carts piled high like peddlers
on endless prairie.

I think about this, sister,
as I scrub my hands
and don the yellow gown and gloves
to enter your room,
you, stuck here all week and worse
to come.

Your nurse is foreign,
difficult to understand, you tell me,
but she sings, *Que sera, sera,*
you join in, *whatever
will be, will be*

2.
I freshen the water in the vase,
pick out the gerbera daisies
once so erect, take a sharp cut
to what remains, nothing

like the original, the red
and gold of autumn,

for who would send you pale blossoms,
you who never ordered vanilla
in your life,

your life narrowed to this room.
Finally I sit, summon the will
to look you in the eye:

"How are you, today?" You answer, "Do you want
a cookie? Someone brought cookies."

3.
Winter trees in the park
are most beautiful
at twilight, half-light.

Everything soft,
slow. Today's snowfall,
complete.

I feel the old pull of landscape,
my eyes wanting
to rest there.

But you are waiting
in your last home,
and walking into the center,
I feel the quiet of the corridors,
night coming on.

4.
I'm high up looking at hills that roll
and undulate a generosity of landscape
a million trees   I wonder   do trees
have souls   do we   is there any
sense in which   sister   you are still
alive   when I see the big picture I think of you
the way I did last Friday   I turned on
PBS before *Mystery*   there was a singer
in a silver gown baptizing the new music
hall in Kansas City   she opened her mouth
out came "Somewhere Over the Rainbow"
slow   she took   her   time   unreeling
the loneliness of that song   I turned
to call you to say don't miss it sister

5.
The first days
you stuck with me, close,
not your body wheeled down
the hallway on a gurney,
but ghost at my side,
shadow at my feet.

I thought I could leave you
behind for an hour, step
back into my poet life.

During the reading I sat alone
and when it was over moved
from one person who didn't know you
to another: *my sister died.*

Each face flared
as if a match had been dropped.
I couldn't douse the flame.

SOLILOQUY

First the quiet of autumn
with no football
on television,
the hours serene
and lonely, then
my voice goes,
can't talk to the kids
on the phone
at his place,
holed up for days
in the bedroom
that is not quite
my room yet,
bursts of steam
from the humidifier
loosening wallpaper,
peeling away the years
first his things gone,
then the man himself
lost in the vapors.

ROAD TRIP

She drives the Pontiac Executive,
a car so big and battered
that when her brother sees it
he says, "*Where in hell
did you get that car?*"
Three teenage kids;
no harm came to any of them
in the Executive,
a boat that kept them afloat
until times got better.

NEGATIVE SPACE

1.
The dog is dead,
bones buried in the backyard
under the rooster statue.

We live here alone, teenagers gone
with all their electronics.

The maple trees are gone
and so is the shade that stunted
the blossoms.

The great elm down the street is gone
but the sidewalk still rises up
from its roots.

Rudie next door is gone but we have
the cake plate and linen napkins
from the sale.

2.
Subtract the houses sitting
four-square on stone foundations;

Let the steps up to the house crumble
like the wreckage of Pompeii;

The hosta planted everywhere,
dig it up along with the day lilies
that overflow the border.

The blue hydrangea and all
the hybrids born in agricultural schools,
let them die.

We have pruned and cut,
arranged too much.

What did the land look like
before we came, the savannah of oaks,
prairie grass,

then the first shelter,
carved out of wilderness,
brave, that claim,
I am.

THE NEIGHBOR SPEAKS

I'm licensed now. Someone in the neighborhood
reported me to the city. Eleven altogether. Persians
and calicoes, Siamese and their kittens. How did I get
so many? Let me tell you one story. I was feeding this
calico. Every day she came to the door, I let her in, fed
her, she looked around and then walked out. One rainy
night, I was watching the Twins game and I heard this
scratching. I went to the door and there she was with
three babies. I kept them all. I guess she was inspecting
the place, like the city.

I KEEP THEM CLOSE

My life passes before me, minus the trouble.
No photos of sickness or sorrow.

I find tiny negatives of my first wedding,
25 years into the second marriage.

Photos of my brother, face shining in Kodacolor
and yet he is with my *Grossmutter* in her long apron,

with my father in his sleeveless undershirt,
drinking a beer, laughing,

with my mother on the lawn of the farm—
all of them gone from the light.

SINGLE

Just when I had run
out of anger
when I could have lived
years without a man,
raising kids, filling out
forms, (except the night lilacs
broke open
and loneliness pooled
on the kitchen table)
just when the house was tidy,
you came with your dog, Muffin,
(I had never had a dog)
came with books, notes
in bad handwriting,
thousands of papers,
the spine on the book of life
undone.

STEPDOG

I was the only dog she knew
none in the childhood that she remembers.

The best times were riding in the backseat
of the old Plymouth station wagon

spinning down country roads
gravel flying out from the wheels

her face in the fur of my neck
my nose to the wind.

My nose to the wind
her face in the fur of my neck

gravel flying out from the wheels
spinning down country roads

riding in the old Plymouth
the backseat, the best times.

None in the childhood that she remembers
I was the only dog she knew.

MISS POST REMEMBERS

The downstairs unit was empty for over a year after the Nevelsons moved out. Olga was gone too. I kept Olga's room exactly as it was as if it were a guest room. The house was very quiet, but I had my books. I was a medical librarian, so I was used to quiet. Still, I was sitting atop an echoing space, the whole first floor and the basement. Walking down two flights of stairs to do my clothes and the tea towels—I use a new one every day—I could almost hear the Nevelson boy, Teddy, in the back hall calling out to his mother to come find him. I didn't really know children, being single all my life. Olga had a daughter in Wisconsin. We shared the upper duplex for ten years before she died. Toward the end, she went to live with her daughter.

I saw everything going on in the neighborhood through the drapery of oak trees from the front windows—the schoolyard where the children played, the sun going up and down, I saw the truck pull up the day they moved in. The house rattled with shouts of "where does this go?" and a flock of young people, teenagers, and a dog! An invasion it seemed the first months, the sudden smells of pungent spices. It was all noise and then quiet. Sometimes the kids were there, other times they weren't. It was the strangest arrangement. Olga would have caught on long before I did. It was a second marriage and they both had children. The wife's were younger and went back and forth. His were older and on their own. I began to like the rhythm of it, the filling and emptying out, the smell of roast chicken, laughter in the stairwell.

LONDON, ONCE MORE

1.

A gray city for a gray time. The spires of the Houses of Parliament embrace fog. The filigree of bare trees on the boulevard.

January and the wind's up. At home it's snowing or too cold to snow. Away from family, I dream of them, even my dead brother.

That first time, our honeymoon, we rode into Trafalgar Square atop the red bus with giddy pigeons circling Lord Nelson and the bells of Saint Martin's swinging.

In our hotel in Bloomsbury, three stars, one of them broken, along with the lift. You rig the shower. I climb narrow steps to the tub room.

We're here for a spell, taking turns hanging our underwear. We store the wine in the window casement overlooking the British Museum.

A faint must as we enter the breakfast room, where foreign students with elegant manners practice their English. Setting the plate of eggs before us, they say, "thank you."

Each afternoon we empty a drawer and turn it upside down, our table of cheese and crackers, chocolate, wine.

2.
The sun shone for three hours this morning. We
walked to Westminster Abbey where shafts of light
broke up the ancient stone.

Choir boys in red, ushers in morning coats. Crossing
to the bathroom I passed through Poet's Corner,
stepping lightly over Auden.

At the sign of peace, the old sailor, turns a merry eye
on us, offers his hand, says to you, "Hello, luv," and to
me, "Hello, darlin."

I lose gloves, you lose money, we lose each other in a
huge museum. I stand still, eyes like radar, looking for
your red shirt.

I have money, I could find my way back, but what if?
I describe you to a guard—red shirt, white hair, 5/10.
He makes a curve with his arm. No pot belly, slender.

Later, you are pleased with that, after we have both
said, "Where were you?" We are a duet of mistakes,
alone in a city we love.

Phone calls home, their voices, cheerful, bright as
balloons. They ask about your pain. You tell them.

At the British Museum, repelled by the massive figures
from Assyria, I think of Shelley's *Ozymandias,* "Look
on ye works, ye mighty, and despair!"

Cezanne's card players at the gallery. In the dignity of their bearing, like Atlas, they faithfully hold up the world.

We walk and walk. My peasant feet plod on forever, left, right, as long as the pace stays the same.

Recruits in camouflage, off to Afghanistan soon, march through the park, sending pigeons flying in formation.

A woman in a scarlet gown is singing an aria from *La Boheme* by the escalator in Harrod's. Enchanted, I go round and round until the final note echoes.

The ballet, the deep velvet of the curtain, the royal crest. We are perched high above the chandeliers. So many light quick-quicks.

My hair loves London, its moisture. Everyday it looks good. You take my photo in front of Westminster Abbey, arms akimbo, big smile, the best version of myself.

Couples are traveling, almost always couples. Will we come here again? Your pain slows us down. "Still Life with Skull." Too much art.

A singing violin as pure as the human voice, the stirring run of notes and the tenderest of diminuendos. Your head rests against the high bench, eyes closed, smiling.

To Eugene

I crossed the country, flew straight
over the Atlantic to Madrid,
another plane to Alicante
where a courtly man drove with skill
up and down mountains to the artist house
on Carrer Mare De Deu
where I was welcomed and shown
a room with a single bed
in which I slept through the bells
of Saints Cosmos and Damian
(and the rooster) straight into Sunday
to find the one public phone in the village
along the flank of the church,
and with the noon blaze full upon me,
fished my telephone card
(five euros, 50 minutes) out of my purse,
the salt of sweat blurring my vision,
punched the numbers,
the English number,
the PIN number and your
number which is our
number and got it right.
Hello, you said.
Hello.

VETERAN

1.

I'm used to it now, a hospital the size of the Pentagon,
but in the beginning I thought it would swallow my vet,
so much bigger than any individual.

That flag in the atrium hanging from the ceiling
with five floors squared around it, big as a rambler,
as a football field.

I can still get lost among the floors sprawling at an angle.
You have to stick to the alphabet and not go off on a hunch.
I know the waiting rooms—nuclear medicine, emergency,

intensive care, cardiac. I've waited with the others,
women from small towns on the prairie who got up
at first light to drive their vets toward scrutiny.

The waiting is long. You can break up the time shopping
in the PX, looking over socks, candy, padded bras, emollients,
knit shirts in XXXL, decals, all the essentials.

2.

The first time in the emergency room, it was hard to find
a phone to call the children to come, and quick.
You recovered. I bought a cell phone.

When Obama took the oath, the drums of the nation
pounded. I waited in cardiac, watching the television
as a doctor threaded a catheter through the top of your leg.

The floor cleaner rumbled by with his machine as big
as a tank. Doctors, nurses stopped to watch the television.
When the nurse called, I left my fellow Americans

to hear that blood was flowing freely through your arteries.
A bird took flight in my chest. I leaned down
and kissed you soundly. "We go on! We go on!"

3.
People who salute the flag go here. If they're bitter
about their injuries, they don't say it; they go directly
to physical therapy and pull themselves up by pulleys.

I don't know where the women are who served.
For now, it's men who are here and their women,
heading home after plenty of waiting.

On the way out they pass the statue of Bob Hope
which is unfortunately short, as if to take him down a peg,
the man who entertained soldiers during World War II,

Korea, Vietnam and all the years in-between.
We're heading home too; I'm driving, negotiating
the nexus of roads where too much comes together,

all the space eaten up, the vast medical center,
the international airport and the cemetery for vets,
hill after rolling hill of white stones.

BEFORE IKEA DELIVERS THE BED

I'm cleaning out under the old
futon before the new bed arrives,

finding things—back scratcher,
cough drops, a foil Easter egg.

I'm thinking about the number
of times we met halfway,

the movies we watched in bed,
the nights of disturbed sleep,

snoring, nightmares,
coughing fits, pain.

Seventy two hundred sleeps! Ah!
Let it go, let it take its place

in the artifacts of our life,
only stay by me.

To Stay the Changing

I love the back and forth
of the days, home
and not home,
going out but pulled back
by an invisible tether.

How to bear the death to come.

You look older today;
I feel my own jaw slacken

and kiss you more often.

THE SNAKE SPEAKS

For awhile, we were so
happy, and why not?
Paradise! Everything
utterly beautiful, she
most of all.

I followed her
in the garden, there was
a sympathy
between us. She was
playful, laughed easily.

I don't mind taking
the blame, but she
didn't *want* to obey.
Why not call it courage,
the thirst for knowledge?

For a time, it was
paradise. I miss her.

UNIVERSAL DONOR

No one will get sick from my blood.
I have the best blood, prize blood,
O negative blood.

I started donating when my brother
needed pint after pint, although
he didn't get my blood.

I don't donate every 56 days
and sometimes I think
I've given enough.

It's fine to be a universal donor
but it's not as if I'm helping
my brother, I'm just adding

to the walk-in refrigerator with units
of blood immaculately given
and sorted by type.

The room of the gurneys is quiet today,
the nurse relaxed as he swabs
my arm with iodine.

I start rolling the gauze back and forth
in my hand helping the flow
along; the nurse talks easily,

he tells me that my blood
will be used for newborns.
The movie projector in my mind

starts rolling: I've had three newborns, I saw
their spidery blue veins, I know
they were born too soon, even full-term,

too delicate for this world.
I watch the bag filling,
the bag of my blood

so like the shape
of the heart
pumping, pumping.

WORKOUT

1.
I walk quickly to the first machine, scanning the room. I know
few names though I've been coming for years to keep my bones

from thinning. (Why do bones thin and everything else
thickens?) We're all working to keep from slipping further.

The woman on the stationary bike is over 100 and that's
Jason coming to escort her to the chair exercise, offering
his arm like a groomsman.

See the woman in a veil working the pedals in her long
skirt? She watches me in the mirror to see how I work the
machines, not staring, polite,

the way I learned when I was too shy to ask. One time she set
off an alarm in back by the treadmills. She looked scared,

called to the staff who hurried to her. The man in the
orange muscle shirt, said, "Learn to speak English!"

I said, from the low row, "She did!" and went on counting.
One woman was kicked out, for what, I don't know, but
the last time I saw her

she told me, loudly, eyeing the man who had just wiped
down his machine, "I wouldn't trust that it's clean."

Mostly though, we're friendly, a bit narcissistic, trying
to stay as strong as possible. We feel superior in January
when the machines hum

with strangers aglow with resolve, but by the end of
February we have the room to ourselves again, the talk of
winter vacations, an unexpected surgery.

One of us shows up very thin and wearing a scarf on her head.
The next time she doesn't bother and works out bald.

A few more times and she's gone. Nobody says anything.

2.
Very quiet today. I go about my routine, working through
the resistance, cheered by the woman in the pink jacket at
the front desk who greets everyone.

A clerk brings her a tall package stapled at the top. I move
toward the free weights, closer to the front.

She tears off the layers of paper, uncovers a bouquet of
flowers in shades of red and yellow, frothy greens and
spikey ferns.

When she reads the card, she smiles. I'm finishing up
abdominal curls as she crumbles the paper and adds waters
to the vase.

As I leave, I say to her, "You have an admirer." She is rosy
with pleasure, a source of light in a room of machines and
the hum of daytime television.

She says, "Yes, I do."

MONDAY

In the schoolroom with two clocks,
bird song and gears without a face,

the boys and I are writing. They have stopped
their whines and whys, have settled into

Where would you live if you could?
We all write and it is *quiet,* the scratches

across paper. They stop. Erase. Flick
the dust off and continue in the room of two clocks.

When they finish, they come, one by one
to stand by me while I read. Then I look up

into their beautiful calm eyes and ask,
Do you have family in Chicago, in Atlanta, in Miami?

On Mars, in the jungle, in Oklahoma? A mother
four states away, a father unknown? They do.

One tells me the weather is perfect in Chicago,
Another that you live longer if you live in Rio de Janeiro.

I say no, you don't, but do you know the statue of Christ
in Rio and two boys grin and open their arms wide.

POETRY IN THE DETENTION CENTER

We come from our separate compartments,
they from their carrels,
I, from my usual routine.
We form a circle, except
for the young man next to me
who turns away.

I read poems,
they read, taking turns, shy,
then surprised at the voice
that emerges,
a hoop of language, a circle
of light compared to the concrete blocks
of their confinement,
every pencil numbered, every
fork counted.

The door of language swings open,
breath warms
the circle that begins
where it ends
and goes round again.

We sit in the circle and read and breathe.

PROPHECY

His red jumpsuit is startling against his skin, a dead
giveaway. He's defiant, snarls, his whole life
coming down on one assignment. The teacher raises
the walkie-talkie, calls for help. Backup arrives,
a muscular man with a calm voice. He talks softly
but the young man raises his hands, "I'm not going
easy." Except for the crackling of the walkie-talkie
calling security, the room is intensely quiet. Then
the back-up man asks us quietly to leave the room
and we all file out. We stand in the hallway as other
men step into the classroom. No one speaks in the hall,
except one boy who says, "Something's up." The air
is tight, it's pressing against the walls of the hallway.
I can see the other classrooms carrying on absurdly,
students nodding as the math teacher mouths formulas.
We hear nothing from our room, so I picture him red
against their blue, dark against their dark and light,
a depth of force so restrained, the building is in danger
of exploding. Moments pass, then, orderly, as if nothing
unusual has occurred, the men file out, the young man
in red among them, neutralized, neither smiling nor
scowling. They leave; we file back into class to finish
the assignment. At the end of the day he comes back
for his book, bristling, nerves raw. He leaves in a wake
of turbulence. I say without knowing I have spoken:
"Profoundly discouraged."

HOLOCAUST MUSEUM

We walk the gardens verdant
with herbs and flowering trees,
shaped by walls of names of those
who did not forsake the Jews.

We leave as we came, behind
young Israeli soldiers
boarding buses, rifles clanking
at their hips, who see

as we do, the railway car poised
on a cliff, half over the edge,
a stop-watch of disaster,
the Jerusalem forest below,
its unexpected green.

PINK ROSE IN A SLIM GREEN VASE

What told the stem
to stop
and pink to start
curving into hips
heartbreakingly
full?

On the television news,
disaster.
my life:
the world breaking,
rhapsody of the rose.

NUMBERING THE OAKS

1.
I am the sweeper
of acorns on the sidewalk
brown with tannin,
the one gathering up
bones after the storm,
the burden of oaks.

2.
My mother-in-law
died on the eve of Halloween.
In the long raking
of leaves, I laid her to rest,
wind sharp around my shoulders.
The comfort of oaks
still standing.

3.
I studied Aristotle in college,
baffled by *treeness, essence of trees.*
I thought I would understand it
by the time I was a senior.
I gave it up for sex
and babies.

Now I understand
with my body—
eyes, tracking the trail
of bark from trunk
to the explosion of limbs;
with my back and hands,
the work of them.

4.
Is it the German in me?
Echo of the forest in the German character
still alive? Lover of trees, of woods.

Every year I grow more attached
until now I am spinning
myth, how they arise
from roots deep in the earth yet fly
into air; how they lose
their innocence in rain
and turn sexual;

but in winter, oh, winter,
without the distraction of leaves
oak trees whisper like giants
to heaven,
one pure
form to another.

The Tour Guide Speaks

I wish you could see children flooding the lobby
jamming up the line, talking, then raising their eyes
to Chihuly's *Sunburst*, "It's on fire!"

They walk the great hall not staying behind me.
giggle at naked Doryphorous,
mimic his stance, spear in hand.

Dogs in a painting distract them. So do
parquet floors that creak; the brass elevator
they love best. "We're in jail!"

Born in the new century, they take in—
the figure of Venus four thousand
years old, the portrait of *Frank*, 1969.

Wealth built this museum. You come, I come,
but I wish you could see the children come,
our *spes regis,* hope of the kingdom.

ART MUSEUM

In the deep well
of the rotunda,
a voice fades
and I am alone,
walking among
the bleached heads
of Roman magistrates
and Greek athletes
with parts long-missing.

I've left behind
the small rooms
of my life.
I slip through the great hall,
a pilgrim
like the figures
in this Chinese hanging.
They're climbing a mountain,
lost in the inky lushness
of trees, the steep
winding toward
the summit.

Pilgrim, you who love
the intimate,
what do you seek
in the great temples
of the world
in cathedrals and mosques,
in space large enough
to swallow you?

AFRICA

When I first sponsored a child
I put his photo in a frame
on the piano with the other children
in the family, but that boy
disappeared, another was assigned,
then another.

I do not know what happens to the children.
Maybe they grow up.
The thread between us
is thin; nothing I do
does much good.

I have the name of one
boy, Thokozani Miseche of Malawi,
a boy of ten, one of one billion.

His favorite food is bananas,
favorite color red
like the soccer ball he drew.
I can see his smile from my desk
where I write this poem.

THE SHOWING

for Barbara

Full moon bounces on the tips of trees
big and beautiful as we ride home.

Young, I had no use for the moon –
eyes on school, work, falling

in love sans moon, grounded in earth,
babies. What use the moon?

Dreamy come late, come waking
at midnight after she died, first death,

worst death, waking to long filaments
of light. Moon come to me; I almost turn

away, but what use, all my attention
to earth if death can take us so young?

Moonlight singled me out.
I let its veil cover me.

THE USES OF AUTUMN

The oaks have shaken loose their millions.

When I step from the garage on gray afternoons,
the leaves rise up in brilliance.

As girls, my friend and I made leaf houses, marking off rooms,
piles of leaves for the couch, the bed,

a brief career as architects before fathers gathered the leaves
to be burned, our work gone up in smoke.

I comb the earth with long sweeps, leaving
the ground bare and flat.

Above me the limbs of the oak frame the sky,
holding it, day after day. Steady.

COMPLINE

All day the music of the heart failed,
but now deer feed at the edge of the wood.

What joy to see the harvest moon ride the sky.

The deer return to wood's shelter,
and sleep curled around the heart.

So let me sleep tonight, riding the moon's breath.

Index of Titles

ACKNOWLEDGEMENTS

Many of the poems in *Stopping for Breath* were written while I was an MFA student at Hamline University. In that sense, I wrote under the influence of the teaching poets under whom I studied—Deborah Keenan, Jim Moore, and Katrina Vandenburg. That time of intense reading and writing was an incubation, a gift I gave myself years into the love of writing poetry. I am grateful to them for being teachers and companions in writing. Other companions have given steadfast support and helpful readings of my work over the years—Sharon Chmielarz, Kate Dayton, Barbara Sperber, Margaret Haase, Roseanne Lloyd, family and friends, in particular, my husband, Eugene Jax. Writing poetry is the way I make sense of the world. Thanks to all of you for helping me on my way.

A special thanks to John Toren, who designed this book, and to Norton Stillman, publisher of Nodin Press, whose lifelong commitment to books and publishing has so enriched our community.

Thank you to the editors of the following publications where a number of these poems first appeared: *Commonweal*; *Lalitamba, Sleet Magazine; Saint Paul Almanac; LIEF; J Journal, New Writing for Justice; Rock, Paper, Scissors; Whistling Shade; Stone Voices*.

Norita Dittberner-Jax grew up in the Frogtown neighborhood of Saint Paul, amid a lively mix of German, Irish, and Polish neighbors. That early blending of ethnic cultures struggling for footing in the middle-class influenced her later work as a teacher and a writer. Her family was large, musical, and politically articulate. She grew up with a firm grounding in the real world and the desire to be part of a larger community, two themes that make their way into her poetry. She studied English literature and education at what is now Saint Catherine's University. She was a teacher of young children, an urban high school English teacher, and a teaching writer for COMPAS. It was only after she finished teaching full-time and had published three collections of poetry that she entered the MFA program at Hamline. Norita lives in Saint Paul with her husband, Eugene Jax. The time they have spent traveling has been a rich resource for her writing. Her work has been recognized by the Minnesota State Arts Board, the Jerome Foundation, the Loft Mentor Program, and the National Endowment for the Humanities. She is one of the poetry editors for Redbird Chapbooks.